# Flickering

# Flickering

PATTIANN ROGERS

*with a special section by*
JOHN A. ROGERS

PENGUIN POETS

PENGUIN BOOKS
An imprint of Penguin Random House LLC
penguinrandomhouse.com

Page 91: J. A. Rogers et al., "Soft, Curved Electrode Systems Capable of Integration
on the Auricle as a Persistent Brain–Computer Interface," *Proceedings of the
National Academy of Sciences USA* 112(13), 3920–3925 (2015).

Page 92: J. A. Rogers et al., "Three-Dimensional, Multifunctional Neural Interfaces
for Cortical Spheroids and Engineered Assembloids,"
*Science Advances* 7:eabf9153 (2021).

Page 93: J. A. Rogers et al., "Injectable, Cellular-Scale Optoelectronics with
Applications for Wireless Optogenetics," *Science* 240, 211–216 (2013).

LIBRARY OF CONGRESS CATALOGING-IN-PUBLICATION DATA
Names: Rogers, Pattiann, 1940– author.
Title: Flickering / Pattiann Rogers.
Description: First. | [New York]: Penguin Poets, [2023]
Identifiers: LCCN 2022041770 (print) | LCCN 2022041771 (ebook) | ISBN
9780143137665 (trade paperback) | ISBN 9780593511787 (ebook)
Subjects: LCGFT: Poetry.
Classification: LCC PS3568.O454 F65 2023 (print) | LCC PS3568.O454
(ebook) | DDC 811/.54—dc23/eng/20220831
LC record available at https://lccn.loc.gov/2022041770
LC ebook record available at https://lccn.loc.gov/2022041771

Printed in the United States of America
1st Printing

Set in Carniola with Griffo Classico
Designed by Sabrina Bowers

This book is dedicated to the readers, those in the past, those today, those tomorrow, always into the far future, and dedicated to all writers, the authors, the poets and their words, and the making of the books, editors, printers, publishers, and dedicated to the lyricists, and the listeners listening in audible, in digital, the words spoken out loud or whispered or sung, solo or chorus, or, in silence, the words touched as braille, as well, dedicated to all tenacious words indoors, outdoors in forest shadows, and breezes, and rains, on ocean sands, to the audiences in auditoriums, in chapels, this book is dedicated to all, readers, writers, listeners, and words, *Flickering*, my book/your book, dedicated forever.

✳

## For the Song Delivered and the Moments Left

Once I watched a flame flickering in a fire
circled by rocks. It was singing in a melodic, foreign
language. The humming cadence of its quiet sizzle
sounded occasionally as the flame was swaying,
dimming, uttering a soft, breathy click, one castanet
tap, then a rush of light, golden and alive with intention.
A spark, a tiny sun flew into the night. I watched
the gestures, listened to the words, the flame
faintly flickering still, becoming smaller, weaker,
nearer to earth, transforming itself into a blue pearl
shining in ash at the root, not dead, not alive.
It shivered once, shook itself into breath and out
again into silence and disappeared, and I said
I understood everything.

# Contents

# VORACIOUS

# CREATION IN RECOVERY

# ASSESSING THE SITUATION

# CREATED IN THE IMAGE

# Introduction

When I started writing poems for this new collection, I was using the word *Flickering* as the working title. As time went on, I became quite fond of the word, the look of it, the distinctive sound of it, its carefree music, how it rang at the end and the ringing rang on. *Flickering* suggested a light-hearted stance and a promise to return.

*Flickering* offers writers wide possibilities. It can function as a verb, an adjective, and an adverb (when it accepts an *-ly*). It is a common noun and, with variations, can be a proper noun too. Flicker is a bird of the woodpecker family. In the book *My Friend Flicka*, Flicka is a horse.

In addition, *flickering* offers countless opportunities for functioning as a metaphor.

Another advantage of the word *flickering* is that it instigates happiness in most people when they experience it in action or encounter it in the wide physical world of nature. Why? I'm wondering about this. People call flickering beautiful. It made me happy just to write this list: flickering sunlight on a lake, flickering fireflies, dew flickering on morning grasses, flickering holiday garlands, the gorgeous flickering inside a diamond. Tiny sequins are sewn on clothing so the body can flicker.

So what does *flickering* have to do with the poems in this book? With all of its promising strengths, the word also presents some weaknesses. *Flicker-*

*ing* is defined as being unstable and unpredictable. Something might flick off and then on and then fade slowly away again. During the years when many of the poems in this book were being written, the times were particularly unstable and unpredictable. These circumstances were caused by a world-wide pandemic virus that touched every continent on the planet with its pall.

There was a great deal of uncertainty, death, sickness, suffering, and disruption of settled customs and the habits of normal daily life. I did not want to write poems addressing explicitly these pandemic circumstances. However, I did desire a silent, subtle presence of the pandemic in some of the work. I wanted to write poems that might be entertaining, or calming, or that might offer a respite. And despite the suffering, maybe I could write poems that would evoke a momentary escape, a settled hope, a brief assurance.

The final section of this book contains a prose discussion of an important topic: the flickering electrical waves present on and across the healthy brains of every living creature on the earth. The study of the human brain even uses the name *electronic flickering* for this essential activity of any healthy brain. Still photographs of the essential electrical flickering occurring in a living human brain are presented in this section of the book. The images are explained in a descriptive text and are accompanied by lines from earlier poems of mine describing flickering in nature. The images and texts are provided by my son, John A. Rogers, professor at Northwestern University and director of the Querrey-Simpson Institute for Bioelectronics. Images like these help scientists find ways to aid and heal an unhealthy or injured brain.

This last section is also an example of interdisciplinary work accomplished by two people educated in different fields—a research professor of physics, chemistry, and medicine, and a poet—working together toward a common goal to widen, expand, and enhance our understanding of life.

—PATTIANN ROGERS

# HOMESPUN

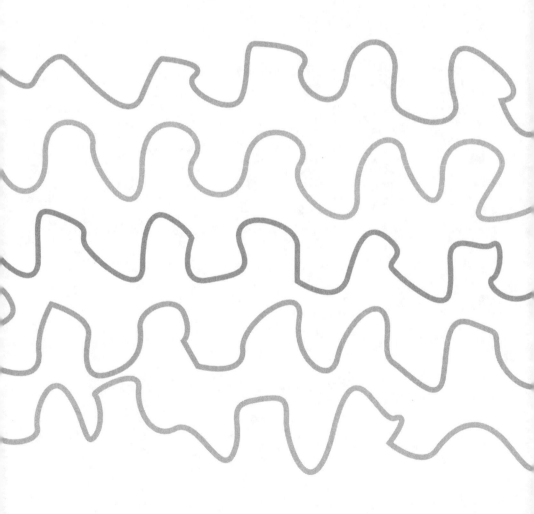

# Summer Isn't a Life-Form, Exactly

However, summer, as itself, has attributes of life.
It emerges when the hard shell of winter cracks
and the infant spring soon becomes summer
fully born. Summer's birthday then is celebrated
like a new child come to the world, galas
of flowers, fetes of color and songs of freedom.

Summer is not moribund like a still pillar
of stone, not a blank, sheer, silent granite wall.
Summer constantly reaches out and inward, as do
we all, with many a variety of appendages surely,
vines, tendrils, limbs, roots, blossoms, searching,
exploring, encroaching on sky and earth, as do we all.

The same as most other life-forms, summer
has a voice, a steady score of tiny taps, bellows,
bell tones, and shrieks, a percussion of clickings
like hidden needles knitting in the beetle-heady
grasses, reams of messages, a diary of summer psalms
(properly translated) winging the sky with song.

Summer breathes a menagerie of fragrances,
juicy berries, red and purple, the scents of warm,
fertile riverside mud, and dreamy memories,
the perfumes of a wildflower-sun over colorful
plains and fields not always seen or found by everyone.

Summer is a life-form, precisely. It lives
with focused intent to its fullness of abundance
and then recedes, as do we all, dying a dreadful
death, withered leaves of maples, oaks, sweet gums,

cultivated violet roses, latticed morning glories,
all reduced to shattered forests and blackened
gardens, summer, stripped of its allure, splintered,
its former radiant presence now sodden refuse,
the remains of summer's once grand being.

But look now at the living summer's dawdling,
how its creek laps and licks the earth, tongues
its sweet and pungent fruits as it passes, dallies
and caresses its tiny waterweeds and swaying
ferns, offering itself wide open. Go ahead.
You know how. Jump right in.

# The Skedaddlers: An Overview

Skedaddling (though the word sounds jolly, flippant,
and funny) is not a happy dance but an urgent flight
from danger, carrying the message "Get out of here fast!"
Almost all living creatures do it, some better than others.

Often just one quick glimpse of one small sliver
of a snake can be seen as it skedaddles. A flicker,
maybe only the tip of its tail is sighted slipping
under a rock silently and quickly as if it were liquid,
or totally disappearing into a maze of weedy grasses
the exact color of sun and snakes. Did I see a snake?

Although somewhat awkwardly, geese are easily seen
and heard skedaddling, running across their home lake,
making a huge commotion with fearful squealings
and squawkings and flappings before they can manage
to wing into the freedom and safety of the welcoming sky.
I do think geese deserve compliments for this escape,
as it seems rather difficult for them to accomplish.

There is a debate about which are better skedaddlers,
squirrels or rabbits. I say squirrels, because they can skedaddle
around and around the trunks of trees and suddenly appear
like trapeze artists on a swaying branch at the top—champions!—
their tails flipping wildly through their chittering and taunting
of the dog barking below. I can excuse this discourteous
bragging, considering the circumstances.

But then nothing can match in speed the quick, sharp
turns, the split-second complete reversals in direction
that a white rabbit can perform skedaddling when chased

by a ravenous fox across a snowy field. I might say the fox
is skedaddling too (however, that's not technically accurate).

Strangely enough, I've witnessed clouds skedaddling,
racing through the sky in an angry wind, altering
their shapes like ghosts frightening all life below,
old and young, their shadows looming over wretched
drying grasses and frizzled-up willow bushes that can
never skedaddle on their own, unless they are broken off,
uprooted by the wind, and sent rolling across dusty plains,
bouncing down highways as tumbleweeds, which are
the very weak cousins of genuine skedaddlers.

It's a most exciting event whenever gazelles skedaddle.
If the swift beauty of gazelles fleeing on the open savannas,
over grasslands and deserts, weren't instigated by fear,
there would be applause, awards, and accolades given
for the adroit leaping and stotting, the perfectly executed
pirouettes, stamina and artistic grace of their svelte bodies.
They are greatly admired, almost magical, as are all
skedaddlers, so magnificent in their terror.

# Of Rivers or Trees?

Some people might admire rivers more than trees
(rivers washing as they do all day and night
and being cleaner than trees that are always
dropping their seeds and shells, the dead parts
of themselves to the ground, creating a roughage
all around in plain sight).

But rivers are somewhat bland, rarely possessing
a distinct color of their own, primarily reflecting
the tints and shades of living landscapes nearby.
In summer, rivers appear like the summer skies
at noon above them, later assuming the fiery
scarlet-russets of evening, as if believing all along
they were the times and skies themselves. Rivers,
unlike trees, multiply the beauties around them,
reflecting the blossoms of sweet flag, hempweed,
indigobush, mimosa blooming along their shores
and borders, and at night transforming the one
full moon into thousands of moons flickering
on the wavering ripples.

One doesn't often hear a tree calling in the distance.
Although once, in a windy hardwood forest, I thought
I heard "oak" slowly being sung in the deepest, fullest,
bass voices rising up from the earth to surround me,
and a whistling soprano "suuuumac" coming
from the open foothills, accompanied by a whispering
"ceeceecedar" in the background for rhythm. (My blind
friend told me that he'd heard these trees long before
I heard them. I do trust my blind friend.)

In contrast, rivers are nearly always easy to hear,
rowdy, roaring and racing without pause, rising up,
crashing over boulders and down on the other side,
slapping and slopping the shore. Rivers can rage
against their banks and other impediments, speeding
past windblown trees and trembling tents tied down
in campgrounds during midnight lightning, thunder,
and relentless rain.

Yet these same rivers, flowing slowly, repeat over
and over the comforting phrases of ancient lullabies
everyone knows. Rivers are often saviors declaring
clearly and definitively to anyone wandering lost
in the plains or forest, "Follow me, follow."

During subzero winters, however, rivers and trees
both are almost totally silent, except for sounding
an explosive crack, a sudden and painful breaking
of ice or branch, echoing through the frigid forests,
near and far away.

Because they swim and feed in rivers, most water
turtles, cooters, musks, don't like trees so much, unless
a large poplar has fallen into the river and become
a perfect spot for sunning turtles. But birds, nearly
all of them, love trees, even tom turkeys. I wonder
whether geese, swans, and ducks might love rivers
and the lakes that rivers create better than trees.
Maybe most birds, overall, love the sky even more
than they love either rivers or trees.

Rivers and trees seem equally self-confident, forging
their own paths through life, establishing trails
over the earth or spreading in patterns against the sky.
A kind of predestination . . . they both seem to know
from the beginning where it is they must go.
And lo, they go that way until the end.

# Coyotes, Chicken Hens, and Spring Peepers

On a clear April evening of a slowly darkening
earth, do we long to listen to a screeching, raucous,
traveling medley of coyotes proclaiming their place
on the sweet, grassy plains, or chicken hens chortling
a low, humming recitation as they nestle inside
their barnyard sheds, or the choruses of spring peepers
ringing together like the zinging of every new leaf
breaking out on the branches of the river trees,
all giving their first answers to the April moon?

Some people might like the singing coyotes best,
their magnificent howls and screaming scales declaring
to the night in shattering shrieks the essential murder
and sex of the earth. They admire these coyotes
and their bold songs of fierce determination to live
with what the earth demands. But many others
are frightened by such vigorous declarations of life.
They carry weapons to protect themselves, their families,
their animals. They often abhor such coyote songs.

Others might find the soothing songs of chicken hens
appealing in their calm acceptance of the stalking
night. The hens are afluff and afeather scratching
their straw, rearranging, preparing, all the while
murmuring to themselves, mumbling to their community
with unquestionable faith in the morning to come.
Many people call hens stupid for being so gullible
and trusting. These people may never love or respect
the chickens' "phony" lullabies in any way.

Those who seek the ringing bells of the tiny peepers
claim they are engulfed by this steady music coming
from the vernal trees surrounding them, and they describe
how the music enters not only their ears; they swear
to feeling the joy in each note of the peepers' melodic
pleasures and desires entering their hearts, trembling
their souls. Yet some people say the peepers just make
a constant clacking racket all night, over and over
the same measure, the same message, never ceasing.

Not often are coyotes or barnyard hens or spring peepers
actually seen at midnight. But all of them can be heard
declaring their presence in their own renditions.
Do we really want to listen to any of them? Or maybe
the song we would like best to hear on a disappearing
April day is not one of the choices offered in this poem.

# Lifting the Soles of the Feet to the Sky

Normal creatures do it all the time—grizzlies
alone on their backs in the soapberry patches
or rocking in the nodding trillium and fragile
bluebells of spring holding their crusty black
pads heavenward, and old cats, matronly lionesses
full of feline reeking, roll in the gritty dawn dust
of the Serengeti, powder their hides, rest momentarily,
eyes dozing, under-paws and bellies fully revealed
to the sun.

Mares and stallions, those leviathans, lie down too
on summer evenings, twist their rumps in the purple
pasture grasses, aim their hooves at the highest
point of dusk or moon. They pause, rhapsodic,
long necks stretched backward, snouts upside down
in the sweet white clover.

Blatant, daring, vulnerable acts of exposure, almost
embarrassing—why should evolution have favored
those performing such silliness? Yet out of the hump
and knead of the surf, out of the white buffet
and draw of the tide, onto the wide, silty sand,
even the ancient sea elephant turns deliberately
belly-up on the beach, the dark pock of his navel
plainly visible, stubby appendages stretched
in obvious satisfaction toward space.

Maybe it's just a practical routine, to cure an itch,
or to rid annoying insects. Or perhaps the light
of the sky touching the belly and the undersides
of the toes actually creates a lasting alloy in the bones,

or maybe the power of a pure, ridiculous delight
like that simply promotes an enduring union of soul
and principle in the blood. Joy has power in the body.

Certainly, then, we should pray for strong, shining
children still rolling and tumbling a thousand years
from now, shouting across the hillsides, pausing
on their backs in the blue abundance of the evening
to lift their bare feet straight up toward the bottom
of morning, toward the first clear star of the night.

# THE BEST OF BONES

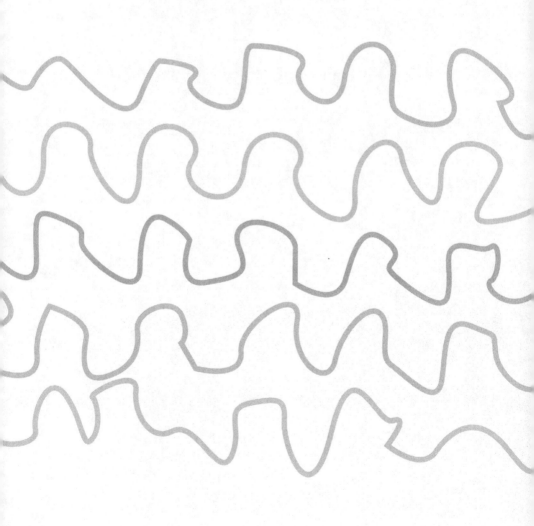

# From the Beginning

Bones have taught us about scaffolds,
the importance of inner framework, balance
and movable levers; by demonstration
have borne testimony to knobs, joints,
sockets, and junctions.

Consider the virtues of bones, the daunting
functions of the protective breastbones and branching
ribs of grizzly bears, blue whales, bowhead whales;
the shielding bones of woolly mammoths;
the bony frills of three-horned dinosaurs.

How crucially necessary: the human backbone,
the dutiful brainpan, that steady skull bone
guarding the brain and its soul, the hefty bones
shouldering a sack of grain, or a load of logs
for winter, or a child's sleeping body.

# Multitudes

Bones are legion, skeletons scattered everywhere,
earth-wide—whether the scorched, dried, burnt
bones of rat snakes or rosy boas on desert sands,
their rib bones lying like tiny ripples on the sandy
dunes; bison bones tangled in piles at the bottom
of cliffs where their stampede ended; coyote bones
half-hidden on high mountain plains open to the sky;
in gardens and fields the thumb-sized skulls of voles
and anoles rattled by the slightest breeze, their minutely
hinged jaws hanging open, each spine a string of slats
thin as pine needles, even a kind of beauty, a wing of
gray feathers left on bones spread open like a fan
cast aside on the forest floor. On the plate, in the fire,
under the knife, we have lived among bones since birth.

# Decoration, Worship, and Gaming

Bones have served us, as tools, weapons, needles,
knives, musical instruments, whistles, and worn
as earrings, strung for necklaces, polished as ornaments
for headgear and crowns, sharpened for pins thrust
through lips and noses, the largest of bones and tusks
latched together for shelters and for shields in war.

Imagine how many ancestral bones have been
worshipped, basked in candlelight, steadily
and surely accepting countless prayers surrounded
by a myriad of chants, knocking drumsticks
made of themselves, perfumes wafting
from the swinging pots of burning incense.

Some people believe that the small bones
of knuckles, toes, anvils of the inner ear, shaken
together and tossed on solid ground (preferably
beneath the pale light of a waning crescent moon),
can predict the future by reading the pattern in which
the bones fall. This pattern and its predictions
can easily be deciphered by any person lucky
enough to have learned the language of bones.
However, in some Asian cultures people refuse
to play games with bones for fear of disrespecting
their ancestors. "Toss the bones."

# Omnipresent Stories

Bones permeate our lives like lasting spirits
speaking in archives, primal histories, voices
from the silent skeletons of executed criminals
and innocents, sacrificed infants buried alive,
their bones preserved deep in the solid darkness
of peat bogs. Across the earth, the bones
of leaders, heroes, kings, pharaohs, chiefs,
buried with their rusted crowns; their bones,
covered by tattered garments and tarnished
riches, speak to us today from their damp
caverns, pyramids, majestic marble tombs.

More than merely memorials, bones are maps
of ancient conflicts, records of the location
where each warrior fell during the final battle,
with shattered weapons, armor crushed, trampled,
his fossilized bones exhumed from beneath
the fields covered now with cemetery forests.

Many skeletons of sailors, traders,
pirates sprawl unnamed in the starless
nights of sea bottoms, hulls themselves
among the board-broken hulls and crumbled
eaves of sunken ships, puzzles of twisted
bones, the rotted mast prone on the deck
still bearing the skull and crossbones
of the jolly roger flag, torn, ragged
and ripped, covered with silt, uprooted
seaweed, kelp swaying in the silence,
slowly in a careless current, their stories
remaining untold.

Bones tell the story of a mother's skeleton lying
in opened soil, a skeletal infant lying at her side,
both unearthed from their shallow grave by a flooding
river along the trail, and the wagons moved on.

Ancient bones burned black, known to have been
gathered by prehistoric humans a million years ago,
were discovered recently by archaeologists in a deep
and treacherous cave passage. Burned black for what
reason? Light? warmth? a ritual? cooking? to ward off
predators? The story will be revealed piece by piece
as scientists carefully study the setting and the clues
and the details of the bones.

# The Extinct, Giant Creatures of North America

They were here, all right, the bone-weight,
reek, and sheer of them, the tremor
of their presence stirring in daylit water
or moonlit water—crocodiles with curved
spikes like oxen horns; four-finned beasts
with round elephant bodies, lizard eyes,
rows of razor teeth, necks 23 feet long;
more than their bones alone: creatures
with octopus tentacles on their heads
protruding from long, narrow, shell-like
tubes; and among the marshes, terrible pigs
massive with humped shoulders, tiny rumps,
miniature legs, their lolling warthog heads
half the length of their bodies;

flightless birds tall as cathedral doors,
beaks the size of steeple bells, wind
and glistening sun furling their feathers
just like any other bird's, and herds of camel-like
creatures roaming the land in fog, rain at dawn,
common shadows of clouds moving across
their souls, each with a bulky, two-pronged
club-horn growing straight up out of its snout,
grazers, the prey of saber-toothed cats.

Blood-fear, bolt, rut, birth and birth
and birth, came with the same urgency
to them, the same ferocity to live. Gone,
all of them stopped, skeletons in a city
museum, staring at me, as if I knew
anything about redemption.

# A Remnant

Once, as a child playing in our attic, I found
a small ceramic box forgotten in the dark corner
of a desk drawer. I unlatched the lid, carefully
lifted the white tissue inside to reveal the complete
skeleton of a small seahorse lying as if sleeping
on a bed of cotton. It was more beautiful, more
finely intricate, than any ornament of lace, more
entrancing than any diamond or ruby rock
could be. So far from the sea . . . I looked
a long time, didn't touch, left it as it had been,
closed the lid, whispered a word, lay the tiny
casket away in the dark desk, shut the drawer
to light, still hearing the cresting sea, still
feeling the swell of its current.

# Remember

Alone or not, you yourself sleep
with a skeleton every night, and you carry
each other throughout every day.

Bones remain, fossilized stone, neither body
nor soul, though they once were the keepers
of both. Why a pity? Why a promise?

# The Oldest Story of the Oldest Story

The sound of it is like a wail
or a sudden yelp, recognized
and unfamiliar, as if a feral dog
or bobcat, captured, had been
deserted, chained in its crate.

Its slant is of icy trees in a cold,
cloudy wind, clinking in the way
necklaces hung with silver coins
and roses resound when thrown
on the draped flags of fallen heroes
passing to their graves.

This story suggests like the fragrances
of seasoned meats simmering with herbs
and spices known only to people
living beyond seas never navigated.

And its tendency is of the call
of late afternoon moving across
rain-heavy grasses. It moves through
the streets of distant neighborhoods,
manifold as the shouts of children
playing in the dusk their shadow games
of talent and stealth.

Its narrative, being both dead
and alive, turns and spirals
like a seeded locust pod spirals
continually in the wind, in the same
way the past and the present turn
continually into one another in the telling.

Like a splash heard in the river mist
at night, this story is omnipresent,
without source, jubilant and weary.

Coming from the bottom of the deep
white cave that is the skeleton of each star,
this story is as hollow as a flume of spring
lily in its rise, as rooted in its bounty,
as generative and unlikely as the creation
of its oldest author.

# THIS BEAUTY IDEA

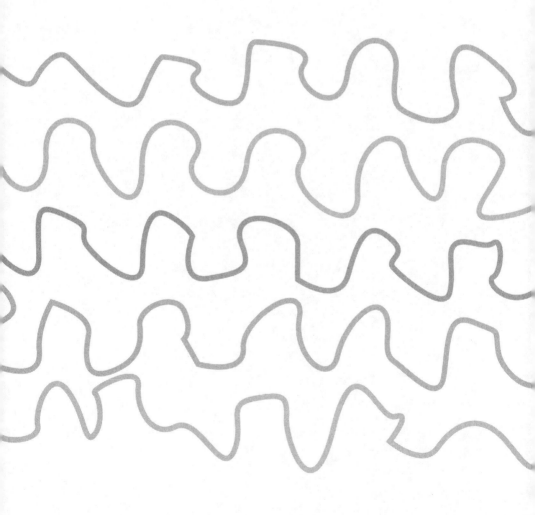

# The Artist

*Landscape with a Pollard Willow*
by Hanns Lautensack

What is it living there among
the jagged shafts, the stripped
stumps and craggy hillocks,
the misbalanced and off-kilter
boulders with their digging lichens,
and there, behind those spears of bare
stalks, inside the mire and mold?

*Watch out! That gravelly slip*
*on the jutting ledge.*

It exists there too among those three
teetering trees in their precipitous
perches. The earth might at any
moment give way, crumple
beneath them, their gnarly stumps
and spikes, matted roots weighted
with dripping dirt, all falling
with snapping cracks and wrenching
moans into the unknown below.

I suppose no one, nothing,
not that distant spire of church
or king, not the near sky above,
would notice or care.

What is it held within and among
these stubs and crooked shafts,
between what has happened and what

has not, this trashy welter of leafy
webs, tangles, rips, tears of torn rock?
What is it living in these lines?

# The Stance, the Stone Statuette, the Sculptor

Not a common stance known already, not a curtsy,
demure fingertips holding the skirt out like sails;
not piously kneeling, hands together at the chin,
lips a silent plea; not standing straight, legs apart,
hands on hips or arms crossed tightly across the chest.

The stance of this white stone statuette is puzzling,
her head tilted back, sideways toward her shoulder,
her eyes averted, aglaze. She holds her open hands
outward close to her waist, palms forward, thumbs
pressed together, fingers spread as hands are often
held before a fire to warm them.

One could suppose she holds her hands to ward
away someone approaching, to shun an annoyance
or ridicule, if it weren't for the lack of curiosity
or anger in her placid face, the disinterest in her
blank eyes, the resignation of her pose.

Today I opened the window facing the field, an early
April morning. I've taken the statuette from the shelf
and placed her on the sill before the scene. I want to see
her stance in stone, her hands held in their usual manner
before a robust background.

The hidden sun hovers, brings easy breezes
of dim lights to blue grasses, wheatgrasses,
still damp from night, the mingling scent of mint,
thyme, fringed sage. Blooms of yellow bells,
common strawberry, lift, quiver here and there
as if in anticipation. A few filaments of cottonwood
seeds float like beatitudes above the blossoms.

A meadowlark startles, calls. Field sparrows flutter
from the rose-crown hedges and disappear. The sun,
now edging the cusp of the earth, comes, spreads
across the field with its one loud, all-knowing word.

Her poised stance on the windowsill remains
unchanged, perhaps conveying everything about her
that the artist intended of her colorless stone.
Her stance, blank, averted eyes, her hands held
as against some uncontrollably dangerous exaltation.

She will not relent even to the promising sway
of the floating cottonwood seeds, or the word
of the sun, the cry of a nestling, the fading stars,
the disappearing moon, even to him who knew
her too well.

# Keeping Beauty under Control

Always tucking away at it, dividing it
into manageable pieces. "The early light
angles its own straight blue branches
through the morning trees." Held nicely in place.
"The white egrets, perched on the fallen tree, rush
upward suddenly in a singular wind-becoming
body of hundreds." Staid, harmless.

Who knows what might happen if beauty weren't
stopped right there at the edge of the bronze-marbled
sheen of the tree frog's brow, at the break of the iris bud
revolving in violet out of itself into itself released.

Just a brief note, "The orange and pink blur of the fallow
spring field passing; the finely tied and self-motivating threads
of the yellow mayfly," and that's enough.
*Restraint* is the watchword.

Because, on a night like this, when the moon is caught
in ice at the far end of its white tunnel, and space
is deepened further in a sky already infinitely deep;
when each dry leaf shifting on the ash tree beside the road
sounds the exact color of its name, and frost on the edges
of the weeds makes jagged lines against the black,
and one might believe it possible to touch the precise
death of every insect lost in the field; then I know
if I'm not careful to look away at the last moment,
to turn back deliberately into some abstraction, I could be
caught up, taken, lost forever, forgetting everything
in a possible consciousness of my own that's waiting,
just waiting for a weakness.

# The Knocking

Sometimes it's like a ticking,
like the ticking metal makes as it cools,
or the random clicking the rafters make
as the house shifts in the wind.

The same insistence is always present,
whether its sound is sharp like a metal ring
rapping at the window or like one loose
shingle flapping directly overhead.

It can clatter rapidly like teeth
chattering from cold, like bones tossed
for a prophecy, like stones rolled
by a current rattling together unseen
over the river bottom. It passes,
as if to reconsider, then resumes
like the tapping of an old man's foot
as he rocks through a summer dusk,
sporadic as the hammering of a woodpecker
in a hardwood forest, first far, then near.

It is reverberant in the tocking sounds
of hail striking rocky ground, the same
sound heard in the ritual languages
of high mountain peoples.

It maintains a constancy like the clacking
wheels of a train on the tracks passing
through the countryside, or like the rhythmic
catching of wheels in a clock passing
through time as if it were a landscape.

Something abroad is knocking.
Something pervasive, resolved, unknown,
seeks entrance. Imagine unlatching
the gate. Envision what may pass
through among us. Pretend to answer.

# The Artist, the Poet:
## This Beauty Idea

The woman sitting poised, erect,
her fingertips barely touching
the strings of the lacquered lute
balanced on her lap, is an abstraction
of beauty in its concrete form.

The water willow in spring, moving
into its whorled leaf, is only one line
in the ever-multiplying propositions
of beauty, just as the river snail
in its whorled shell moves constantly
into the abstract beauty of its own motion.

The poignancy of white egrets in flight,
their long, thin legs vulnerable and intentionally
held against their bodies, is impossible outside
the word *beauty*. There the egrets reside,
stationary in their descending glide over water,
kept forever inside the boundaries
of the eternal abstraction.

Born from beauty first, then found
as autonomous in canyons of pinyon
and juniper, the amber lily becomes
the abstract notion of itself embodied
in a particular direction of orange,
a specific star-structure of bloom.

A statement of beauty in the abstract
might itself possess beauty were it set

to music and sung on an early summer
evening among weighted grasses rising
to broken light after rain.

Be my idea, my own  .  .  . beautiful swave
of silver trout, beautiful purple iridescent
barb of pointed bunting, radiant violet dragonfly,
wind-across-moon of beauty, template of red
rock cliffs and sky. Be my beauty this moment,
thus abstractions of beauty spoken, touched,
real, and living.

# The Beauty of Harps and Bells

Bells come in a greater variety of sizes than harps do.
Some bells are as small as acorns or pearls, a few
so tiny they possess only sparks of sound barely heard,
like snowflakes.

Bells can be gigantic and shocking, so large
they must be transported place to place by a flatbed
truck and then lifted by a crane to their homes,
often at the top of cathedral steeples. A bell this large,
when tolled, can challenge and outdo even thunders
of gods rolling and echoing over the countryside,
capturing the attention of the populace, scattering
frightened birds, children, and small creatures in all
directions. (Big bells always win.)

Yet even a small harp (lyre, zither, or Celtic)
possesses a versatility of tones from treble to bass
that a single bell alone can never replicate. Many
musicians truly love harps, as demonstrated by the way
they put their arms around them, rest them on their
shoulders and hold them close to their bodies while
lightly stroking their strings. A harp of any size,
even if silent, can be by itself a lullaby of beauty.

Bells are survivors, even though being treated
more vigorously than harps. Bells are shaken
or swung around, strung on necklaces, bracelets,
fastened to the ankles of dancers leaping
and pirouetting onstage. Some bells hanging
from racks are even struck with padded mallets
to initiate their ringing. It makes me slightly

doleful to observe this practice, such a contrast
to the tenderness in which music is elicited
by the graceful fingers of a harpist carefully
plucking and soothing the taut strings.

However, most big bells are honored with ritual
attentions never bestowed on harps. Big bells
are blessed in ceremonies, consecrated with holy
oil, each bell then given a name by its godfather:
Emmanuel, St. Anne, Big Joe, Big Ben, Liberty.
Large bells are tolled in celebrations for royal births,
or when fierce wars have ended. They rang out
from Notre-Dame when Napoleon was crowned.

I don't know if harps are ever given names. If I owned
a small harp and if I could hold it on my lap, rest it
on my shoulder, caress its strings into gracious music,
I would surely give it a name, perhaps after a flower.
Flowers make soothing music too: Sundew, Moonseed,
Morning Glory, Iris, or Orchis.

Once in a small-town museum in Oklahoma I saw
photographs of a beautiful harpist in a white silk
gown who left her home on the plains, became
a success in her time, dancing with her tall, beloved
harp as her partner on stages across the country.
She advertised herself as "a fine lady musician,
with rings on her fingers, her harp in her arms
and bells on her toes, she shall surely have music
wherever she goes."

Both harps and bells give praise to their various gods,
each in its own true, lofty, and authentic ways. Angels
hug their small lyres while floating and flying, humming
hymns above the earth; while hallelujah bell-ringing
dancers join the swirling, circling stars abounding,
ringing with light throughout the night sky every night.

# Amiss

"No, not that shadow moving among the shadows
of the leaves. Maybe there! A wing tip behind the trunk,
the same mottled gray of his feathers? No." The great
horned owl is *gone, missing* again this evening, not resting
in the poplar as was his way all these weeks.

*Missing. Gone. Absent*, closed words, *vanished*
a locked conclusion, *void* a dreamless chill.

The honors bestowed on the poplar have *disappeared*,
no longer to be called the *abode*, no longer the *keeper*,
no longer the dependable *refuge* covering the flutter
of the owl's presence, bearing the weight of his body,
the two merging at moments into one being.

They were a steady endurance whenever a congress
of crows in their glistening black robes circled around
and above the tree where he perched, diving, swerving
up and away, screaming their caws of alarm, alerting
their compatriots to join their attack and routing efforts,
owl-poplar unperturbed by the raucous.

He has *gone.* What occupies his *absence* now,
this *vacuum* nature abhors? A contrivance
of reasoning: "He will come back?" A concoction
of the future: "He will return with a mate and fledglings?"
Memories? all frail, skeletal replicas. A lingering
hope to meet suddenly his golden eyes through the foliage,
gauging again our assessments of each other?

Irretrievable to me now are the words I need
to create his song. Impossible without his presence.

# Stranger and Stranger

I allowed the stranger's stray
cat into my house. She wore a bell
and carried with her the stranger's
sense of herself; searched the premises,
intent, restless, prowling beneath sinks
and the cobwebbed mouse-tangles
of the cellar staircase and its hidden
recesses; leaped up to the wild sunlight
of cedar and oak motion at the window,
she and her bell tipping along railings
and counter edges, sliding past the mosaic
ginger jars on the mantelpiece, dainty
around the ceramic horses, St. Francis
carved in raw wood.

The sound of her bell, soft rattle,
soft as her motion, became the first
living bell of bedsprings, the only
chime among box and chest formations
in the static community of the attic,
the sole tone of tolling brought to silent
cupboards, dull banister pillars.

Pursing, rumpling the chenille bedcovers
and chintz pillows, she stopped once
on our velvet lounge to lounge herself,
stretched shapeless, a boneless bag
of pure somnolence. Stilled and quiet,
the bell became the soundless ring
of her sleep, a sleep so holy and harmonic
it relinquished the name of its host.

She has departed, and now nothing here
is entirely itself, nothing free of cat taint,
cat translation, cat angle and verve.
The tabletop is a cat pedestal; curtain
fringe, cords, ornamented casements—cat prey.

The wood grain of the walls moves like the liquid
motion of cat winding through the empty hallway.
And outside the window where the cat perched
briefly, even the nesting finch I watch is no longer
autonomous, being now, in addition, finch in cat's
eye, the only finch a cat can see.

The corridors and implications of my place, shaped
now by cat present and cat gone, shaped by cat lost
and recovered. Strange reordering strangeness. Come
next time  .  .  .  wolf, butterfly, sloth, slug, wraith, wind  .  .  .

# VORACIOUS

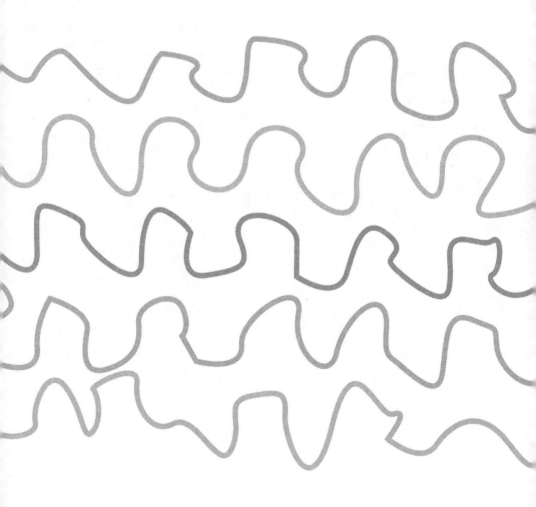

# Archetype II

She couldn't have come from dust
or clay, rock granite, marble,
or ashes; never forged from glass,
that fragility, or fashioned
from any hard mass of a rib bone
still dripping with blood.

Look at her, so clearly designed
and conceived in motion; the lines
of her being were born of the same
river lilt that smooths sharp stones
to perfect orbs, soft opal moons.

She has inherited the caress
and restraint of low waves advancing
in easy turns and glides across a shallow
bay. The mere sight of the slopes
and swells of her body can lull
and soothe a person to peace.

And she moves with the majesty
of deep, downstream meanderings,
calm, consequential. The way
she walks is what she means,
the way water in an eddy or ripple
becomes its own message.

When she shifts her body from foot
to foot she shines with the silver
grace of fish weaving to hold
with the current. She arrived here

knowing already how to stay
with the day moving beautifully
and definitively around her
as they shape one another.

Whether her pathway or her bed,
she intimates and brings forth
with a midsummer measure
of divination and flourish.

She parts mountains. Even in sleep
she multiplies the floating stars,
she, just an afterthought, who never
touched the finger of god.

She is the source that wakens seeds.

# Making Love with the Gods

It's solely a woman's pleasure—Leda's,
Mary's—to be sought with divine intensity,
to be taken, enveloped, infused
eventually, to give life
to the deity of that moment.

And they come upon one
with such surprise—the god
of wild prairie gardens, for instance,
subtle yet overpowering with his gangly
magenta sorrel, his stiff corn-blue
pokeweed and spiny spring teasel,
all of his smothering tongues probing,
nudging, nibbling at once. Those countless
sun-sucking buds and hard, bristled nips!
What a delirium of green blossoms
to be filled with the wind-razzle
energy of his summer straining
stems and stalks!

And I remember the god of rivers,
all day and all night, as insistent
and swift and fragrant as glacial melt
in high meadows, surging forward,
rumbling bottom boulders, rolling,
tumbling, filled with a balm like weaving
slips of a thousand passing fish,
like the smooth rub of quivering flank
on flank. Wasn't the entire sky tilted,
spun, carried away by the rippling beauty
of his bronze-silver flesh? Who could resist

the virtuosity of his bluebead lilies lulled
in quiet inlets or the skill of the piercing cave
swallows darting down his canyon corridors?

There must be a sister somewhere
who can recall with me the mastery
of the lord of snow at night, how one
walked out deliberately and stood
alone dressed in red wool in the middle
of the white, unbroken fall of field
and sky, how irresistible it was to lift
one's naked face and throat to the stings
and caresses of his unrelenting seduction,
to lie down where he wanted, suspended
deep inside that dark drift, to taste,
to drink the clean ice of his higher heavens.

And each time, when one woke afterward,
carrying in the body that same warm,
demanding seed of pulse and pressure
and dogmatic declaration, then no one,
not even envious devils or indifferent
saints, could ever deny or diminish
a love like that.

# The Perfect Lover

Be brave, be skilled, the one who rappels,
draped with rings and double ropes, kicking
away down the mountainside named for you.

Be pale, shriven too, shrinking in a crumpled
white linen suit beside your tea table in July
under a striped beach cabana.

Bring red grapes in a muslin bag
when you come. And bring half a cow
roasted, balanced on your shoulder.
In your spotless spats and vanilla suede
gloves, carry sugar lace and vials of rose
water, jujubes and cherry brandy.

Wear tight leather trousers and rattlesnake
armbands. Wear a silk kimono lined
with violet velvet, appliquéd with satin willows
sewn with silver threads.

Shirtless, just in off the harvest, wear wheat dust
and sweat, wear grain gravel in your hair.

Be fire eater. Be flame chewer. Suck smoke.
Suffer. Burn. Blow frost, implacable,
unmoved, a cylinder of ice buried
in furry sawdust.

Be bold. Before crowds, in a loincloth, swallow
brass swords with musk/horn handles from Asia.
Squat, at the same time, in rat feces, hidden

among the balcony audience, thumbing
your nose at the stage.

Be embarrassed, be fumbler, be novice.
Be virgin. Be slick, seasoned, oiled
and patted with aphrodisiacs, smoothed
in particular places with opium cream, all over
with sweet plum blossom and emerald jelly.

Be Moses. Be Buddha. Be saved. Be God,
Beelzebub gaping, straggly goatee, a sharp,
diamond barb stuck in your navel.

Disappear. Don't exist.
Come back tomorrow night.

# Poverty

The lament wasn't in the stiff
whips of willow or the ice captures
of pondweed and underwater tubers,
as we expected. No moan rose
from the frost-blackened spikelets
of bluejoint or twisted cattail,
no wail from the ice-glassy weeds
fallen, brown, prone in roadside
sheaves. Not one request sounded
in the empty, opened husks
of locust pods or the splayed
sheaths of walnuts and hickories.
The cold fog was almost blissful,
motionless, amenable among the broken
charlock and bitter cress. And only
multitudes of serenities lay in the snow-
filled nests of departed sora and wren,
in the white fixations of tangled hedges,
there the purity of the deaf, the peace
of blindfolds, the wealth of the unperturbed.

But here in this spring tumult
of magenta sorrel, here in this noisy,
bee-scavenged field of unruly daisy,
wild dewberry, and rue, here is where
all frenzies, despairs, and frantic
beseechings wheel and ravage. Lack
and longing alike stagger and lurch
in the twitching blazes and sky-streaking
screeches of kingbirds, killdeer,
bobolinks, and jays, in the gripping

and mewing, the imploring of nestlings,
micelets, and kits. The beleaguered
starry spheres above are accosted
constantly, assaulted by this vagrant
citizenry of scabbling tongues and toes,
these shakings, tuckings, and snatchings,
the begging, budding fruits of coming
pokeweed, elder, crab apple, and plum.

What gnashings and furies, what demanding,
pleading heart bombardments they all are,
each and every one crying harshly
to heaven—please, now—for someone
equal and mighty to come quickly
and match all of these longing passions.

# Celeste, at the Campfire

"Grizzlies, brown bears, achieve an enormous
height when they stand upright. *Towering* is the word
people sometimes use. Once in an Alaskan airport
terminal I stood before a towering stuffed grizzly,
nose lifted as to catch the wind, as if to gauge
its clues, still wary.

The top of my head barely reached the place
where I guessed his heart would have been. I might
have heard it, have felt it pulsing, if my ear were pressed
to that spot, had he been alive, had he understood.

Brown bears  .  .  .  their grizzly brown fur
sometimes reflecting sunlight, flickering golden
like decorative stars through the shadows of pine
trees moving with the forest wind.

I wonder what it would be like to meet
a living grizzly on a lonely trail, watch him rising
slowly, standing upright, nose pointed to the sky,
cautious, but coming toward me then with arms spread,
as if holding the corners of a blanket open, the pure
broad bulk of him unfolding, so fearfully beautiful,
I surmise, so fitting, and then the breath of him,
ripe as raw fish, ripe as fall berries, ripe as earth.

I might have smiled, opened my own arms shaking
in welcome, knowing I was mistaken, knowing
I was wrong, willfully misunderstanding. I might
even have thrown my head back toward the sky,
bared my neck, an offering.

Better, I would think, than on a city street, a steel
blade slicing across my throat, better than fanging
venom in a blazing hot desert, better in a pine forest
than entangled and drawn down into the suffocating
depths of an icy, dark sea, better than a misstep,
a plunge over a high, battering, rocky ledge . . .

In a moment, knowing I was right, at the right
time at the right place unfolding and being lifted
into the mesmerizing light of the body of the right
words released with all the fire of mighty suns . . .
*Ursa Major.*"

# CREATION IN RECOVERY

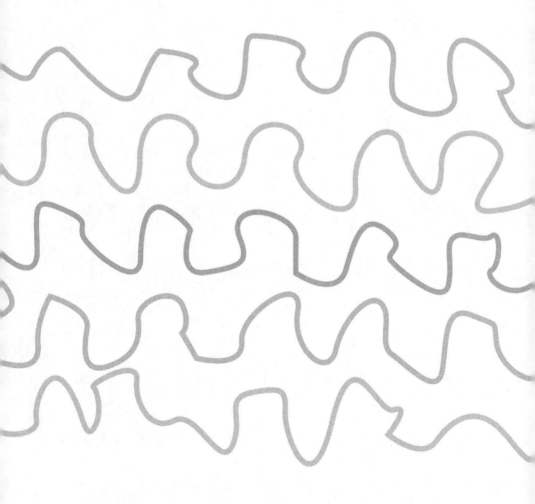

# Convalescence

Please send foreign toys and small goods,
something to amuse and entertain
the sick who languish here,

a piece of prism glass that, without sound
or violence, breaks and transforms
the sunlight as it floats across the walls
through the day,

a twirling plastic moon glowing ivory
in the dark, hanging from a velvet
cord tied to the bedpost,

finger puppets for the energy
of the whimsy—a devil with horns
of felt and a crooked red nose,
a black pig wearing a crown,
the clown of evening with purple
bells and sapphire eyes.

Perhaps send a pellet that resurrects
when dropped in water, becoming
a many-petaled, fuchsia flower
of silk filling the glass bowl,

or even the insensate live—butterfly eggs
in a jar, jumping beans in a round
wooden box;

for faith in the power of the invisible,
deliver 6-inch windmills of silver foil
to spin in the breeze on the open windowsill,

a fan made of translucent shell
that spreads to reveal words written
in an unknown script conveying
by their boldness and slant everything
we have believed with the sick
from the beginning.

# Body and Soul and the Other,
## and the Other

I sit beside the bed, take care, wipe
the perspiration from the forehead,
lotion the breast, oil the dry roughness
of the feet, the scabs of the elbows.

On the table there are tangerines
to suck, small pieces of bread
like communion squares. Though containing
no explicit promises, medicinal teas
are brewed and offered by name.

While tucking the napkin in, I notice
a passing recognition in the eyes.

I open the window, hoping the particle
moments of fragrance in the late velvet
grasses, in the wild mint, or perhaps
the half-tone/over-tone thicket of ancestry
in the call of the wren might enter the room
to establish new arenas of order.

Each leaf-string of the cottonwood
distinguished with wind, the dead dust
of the road resurrected and crazy
with undesigned destinations might
occasion respites.

I promote and soothe, sometimes
with prayers, sometimes recitations.
During spasms I hold the shuddering

shoulders steady. I minister with revival
cadences or a simple gesture reminiscent
of old countries, hair brushed and drawn
back from the face, knitted cap tied
loosely beneath the chin.

Tiring, we recline in silence often,
after the maid leaves with mop,
soap, and towels. Perhaps one of us
will read aloud, head on the propped
pillows, head against the chairback.

When the dull red-orange, looking
like fire behind double silk screens,
disappears from the walls, a colder
sun turns the room to deepening
shades of darker drownings, like blue
lake-light sinking to black underwater,
we hold hands, we sleep.

# The Puzzle of Serenity

In a hard wind like this, a chorus
of monks on the forest path, brown
hoods blown back, white faces bared,
carry their candles cold and dark.

In this rain, in this wind, a fat man
wearing silk bloomers scurries
across the empty courtyard, body
in a forward lean, purple umbrella
popped inside out, yet held, despite,
high above his head.

Those who are incarcerated for madness
stare from behind locked windows,
their glass faces pummeled and battered
by rain pellets, by wet, windblown
leaves and trash.

In such a wind, one must revere
the wild, uncatchable pieces of god's
spirit abominable over the earth,
above waters, and one must believe
the scene painted on Grandmother's tin
handkerchief box—ancient ragpickers
squatting in the dust beside their overturned
wagon, scarves tied across their noses
and mouths, their eyes shut against
the blinding blue desert storm.

Some envision this frightful wind
ceasing and all elements then set right,

the bundles of tumbleweeds, piles
of forest flotsam, dead dried toads,
downed birds, the tangles of torn
papers, all swept with brooms from sills
and doorsteps and crossroads in the calm.

And some imagine the umbrella back
as intended—a small, circular canopy of shelter—
and the wagon upright on its wheels, candles
as candles again lit and burning, the insane
put to bed in peace, and god secure
in his immovable testament, by which means
they may come to recognize broken pieces,
by which means they may come to conceive
a mended whole.

# Never Alone

In a mist-filled forest, below the shelter
of tropical trees, a drop falls, a pause after,
and another drop, and a finger (maybe
the vestige of one) taps with each fall, waits,
the next drop gathers, falls, the tap,
pattering a slow cadence over and over.

I once watched a gorilla, sitting alone
in the corner of his compound, purse his lips
as if to whistle, pull them back in a half smile
showing his teeth, a moment of contemplation,
eyes staring beneath his broad, overhanging
brow, the same silent statement, time by time,
a ritual, a form, stanza after stanza.

Perhaps a hawk whistles a screech. A creature
looks up, imitates the sound, remembers,
repeats it again when there is no hawk, watches
the empty sky become the wing and sound,
the flight, endless, vacant, and pure.

The parched rasp of locust, chirping rattle
of field crickets, dry, burring trills of grasshoppers—
all cadenzas replicated by the human tongue
between the teeth in breathy *buzzes*.
And there it is.

The tongue curled back and rolled forward
sounds the *le, le, le* rhythm of a stream flowing
over stones; a gurgling hum repeats the back-
and-forth *aww-rush* of white river foam
downhill.

I wonder who it was who first plagiarized
the iambic phrases of the robin's song, *cheerup,*
*cheerup, cheerily,* or mimicked the coyote's
octave yips and yaps up and down the scale
of their hunt, the wolf's rising moon-howls
of expectation?

Even an apple hanging from a branch sounds
the solid, committed whole note it maintains
while measuring the time of its ripening.

A flickering of birch leaves in a sudden
swirl of wind—can a dancing voice join in?

Lyric or not, whenever we speak, a congregation
of life and earth speaks with us.

# ASSESSING THE SITUATION

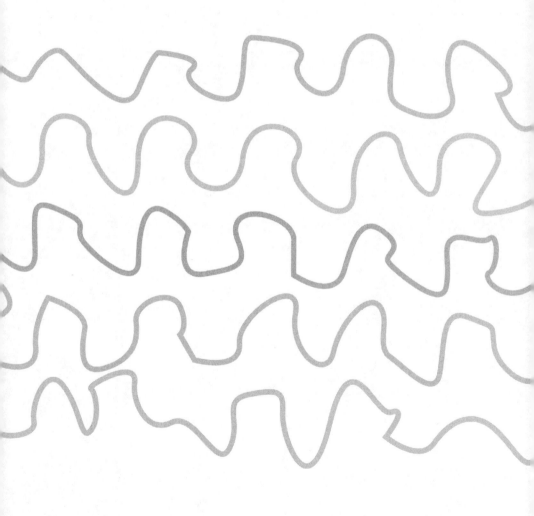

# Assessing the Situation:
## Breath, Spirit, and Chickadees

Breath, blown into the mouth
and nostrils of a swimmer carried limp
from the sea nearly lost, can find,
touch, and waken his heart to life.

Some believe god blew into the nostrils
of the first man created, and he then became
a living soul. (This was once known
as the first resurrection.)

Blown through the lips, blown
through a wooden pipe, a reed,
or the horn of a conch shell . . . breath
can make music just like god
makes a living soul.

Living breath can flutter the down
of a chickadee feather held close
to the face of a sick child sleeping.

But those who sleep in death have
no breath to stir a reed to song
or a heart to life, no breath to raise
a soul, to lift a feather like a poor
birdless wing to flight, to make
music, to sing like god.

If living breath is the holy spirit
of the spoken word (some say twice holy
in prayer), then this invisible spirit

is made visible tonight, an icy wraith,
by the breath of carolers singing
of the Christ in a freezing snow.

Whatever draws breath in a flowering
garden must immediately become one
with the invisible spirit of the fragrant
lily, become one with the fragrant
living soul of the sweetbriar rose.

Some believe the breath from a flock
of chickadees settled in a locust tree
can cause the languid leaves to flicker
microscopically. This spirit is visible
to anyone watching closely enough,
standing still enough, barely breathing.

# Light as Condition

If I had been light once but have since forgotten
that time, I might still be able to understand the white
moth's wing by having previously passed straight
through it in an ivory transformation to the pine needle
bed beneath. I might still understand the feather-legged
spider's web, having been pierced completely once
by the strands of its fragile pinwheel.

And I could comprehend the unabashed orgy
of the horseshoe crabs clacking the salty swirl
of their own semen by remembering when I made
the white seawater that precipitated their first
gathering myself.

I would be able to perceive the pieced and broken
tangle of the forest by recalling the knot
it had once made in my stationary swath.
And I would be able to identify the underside
of anything I couldn't touch by recognizing
the shape its dark vacancy had created
in my presence.

And maybe I could still recall the hard warp of water,
the suck of blackness, and the barrier of mirrors.
And maybe I could recognize bodies by the soft,
definite sculpture of their gravity alone.

And I might remember how to cover every aspect
of the wild meadow rue with the instantaneous
reality of itself, being not the cause but merely
the condition of elucidation evident on the gold-

furrowed pits and hills of the desert dunes,
on the curve of each red spike of the red barrel cactus.

And I might learn how to initiate, by my own
departure, the vibrating stutters of the locust,
the first blooms and bellows of the marsh toads
and mole crickets. I might even remember
how to make an entire darkening, calling slowly,
involuting, shaded expansion of something
like evening possible by the gradual process
of my own inevitable passing.

# In Place, In Time

Someone is standing on a beach somewhere
at the edge where the surf first touches land,
watching the raucous sea, that uncontrollable
beast, rolling and growling, swallowing and spitting,
an unpredictable raptor with genuine weapons.

Its waves race forward, cresting, falling, slapping
a fury of explosions. Seabirds above fly in circles,
calling and screeching. Reflections of the sun shatter
like pieces of glass on the breaking waves. Nothing
pauses even to breathe. This furor stretches to the line
invisible in the far distance where the ocean meets
the sky, where the beast seems to settle, solemn, calm.

Someone standing there watching might begin
to know, might begin to feel in the spine, inside
the heart, at the back of the skull to its utmost extent,
the vision of a never-ending horizon continuing
onward and onward clear to the full curving horizon
of the blue-green earth bold against the black and on
past the slicing white rim of the moon, past Neptune
and the outer solar ring, where, looking back, the earth
appears as the tiniest pearl on the string, bold against
the same endless black where novas, celestial clouds
float in silence, and the open edges of black stars
swallow light and on to that far horizon of time when the
first glint of the first star is just now beginning its travel
toward an earth not yet existing. This vision,
encompassing the light of the soul, is constantly
repeating, "yours forever."

A seabird, a speck of nothing far away, maybe a petrel, maybe a shearwater, might come into view now, rising high out of the horizon and over the wind-tussled sea, its wings spread wide, dipping and swaying with ease above the world, as if attesting to every possibility.

## and the indivisible universe . . .

        and the withered universe
of toad hulls and cracked crust
of winter mushrooms, black fallen
ferns and mildewed cresses and the dead
summer flight of hatchling sparrows
spilled from their field nest in May
and the multiple tits on the breasts
of one-eyed witches  . . .

        and the bursting universe
of ripe plums, bloated carcasses
of drowned cattle and butchered
dogs, the rages and cores of super
novae and hatchet murdered and orange-
white molten rock boiling forth
like day at the night-bottom
of the sea and bedded lovers
in the loving hands of their lovers  . . .

        and the one dizzy universe
of spindles and suns and suns
through swarms of dixid midges, suns
spun by waterspouts and whirlwinds
and circling seeds of green ash
and silver maple and the wheeling
molecules of their varied arts
and equators and suns like circus
rings and ponies tethered like suns  . . .

        and the closed system
of the aerial, arboreal universe

of lemurs, dusky titis, pollinating
bats and monkey-eating eagles,
strangler figs and woody lianas
all twinging, swooping together
with the separate strands of the wretched
universe and the stalwart universe
and the wayward universe piercing
and tangling through the defiant
universe of forest canopies
consequently resulting . . .

and the faltering universe filled
with crutches and braces, rusted nails,
staggerings and stutterings, cement
patches, mucilage, mending rubber glue,
bandages, bolsters and buttresses, putty
paste and the universe of festival
and the universe of faith . . .

and the sublime universe existing
inside the universe of sleep awake
inside the dens of cactus owl and staghorn
beetle nests, pack rat hovels, inside
the buried ova of crocodiles, cicadas,
green turtles and ridley turtles
and likewise inside the biding
of the new moon and likewise
inside the biding of the unknown
existing inside the waking universe
asleep inside the universe
of the sublime . . .

and the moment before the first
categorically seamless universe
of universal categories is acknowledged,
and the moment immediately after  .  .  .

# CREATED IN THE IMAGE

# *Homo sapiens:*
# Creating Themselves

## I.

Formed in the black-light center of a star-circling
galaxy; formed in whirlpool images of froth
and flume and fulcrum; in the center image of herring
circling like pieces of silver swirling fast, a shoaling
circle of deception; in the whirlpool perfume of sex
in the deepest curve of a lily's soft corolla. Created
within the images of the creator's creation.

Born with the same grimacing wrench of a tree-covered
cliff split wide suddenly by lightning and opened
to thundering clouds of hail and rain.

Cured in the summer sun as if in a potter's oven,
polished like a stone rolled by a river, emboldened
by the image of the expanse beyond earth's horizon,
inside and outside a circumference in the image
of freedom.

Given the image of starlight clusters steadily silent
above a hillside-silence of fallen snow  .  .  .  let there be sleep.

## II.

Inheriting from the earth's scrambling minions,
images of thorn and bur, fang and claw, stealth,
deceit, poison, camouflage, blade, and blood  . . .
let there be suffering, let there be survival.

Shaped by the image of the onset and unstoppable
devouring eclipse of the sun, the tempestuous, ecliptic
eating of the moon, the volcanic explosions of burning
rocks and fiery hail of ashes to death  . . .  let there be
terror and tears. Let there be pity.

Created in the image of fear inside a crawfish
skittering backward through a freshwater stream
with all eight appendages in perfect coordination,
both pincers held high, backing into safety beneath
a fallen leaf refuge  . . .  let there be *home.*

## III.

Made in the image of the moon, where else
would the name of *ivory rock craters* shine
except in our eyes . . . let there be *language.*

Displayed in the image of the rotting seed
on the same stem with the swelling blossom . . .
let there be *hope.*

*Homo sapiens* creating themselves after the manner
and image of the creator's ongoing creation—slowly,
eventual, alert and imagined, composing, dissembling,
until the right chord sounds from one brave strum
of the right strings reverberating, fading away
like evening . . . let there be *pathos,* let there be
*compassion, forbearance, forgiveness.* Let there be
*weightless beauty.*

Of earth and sky, *Homo sapiens* creating themselves,
following the mode and model of the creator's creation,
*particle by particle, quest by quest, witness by witness,*
even though the unknown far away and the unknown
nearby be seen and not seen . . . let there be *goodwill
and accounting,* let there be *praise resounding.*

# Poetry, Science, and the Human Soul

W hen I first began to write poetry seriously, years ago, I came across essays published in magazines and journals written by people who were not poets but whose thoughts have stayed with me and influenced me.

One of these essays appeared in *The Atlantic* in 1992 and was titled "The Case for Human Beings," by Thomas Palmer. In a portion of this essay, the author wrote a short summary of evolution in simple, colloquial language, ending with this sentence: "It was as if Nature, after wearing out several billion years tossing off new creatures like nutshells, looked up to see that one had come back and was eyeing her strangely."

That was the beginning of humanity as a wondering, curious, questioning creature; maybe even the first question, a uniquely human invention. Scientists and poets, each in their own ways, still continue asking, exploring, and discovering. Who are we? Where are we? How did we get here? What are our limits? What are our obligations? What does it mean to be human? What is nature?

In his 1973 book, *The Ascent of Man*, Jacob Bronowski (a mathematician, scientist, and poet) wrote, "The underlying essence of science is questioning. Ask an impertinent question and you are on your way to a pertinent answer."

Questioning is also an underlying essence of poetry, poets suggesting, wondering, seeking to understand our reactions, our emotions, the source of the soul and heart of our lives.

I never aspired to be a scientist, but I like listening to scientists talking together (using the pronoun *we* when referring to their research) and so often using the words *suppose, imagine, consider, what if* . . . asking questions and attempting to respond to them through observation, research, experiment, mathematics, curiosity, and imagination. I admire the best scientists for their dedication to their work, their respect and reverence for the natural, physical world, and their required absolute honesty in reporting the results of their research.

After all, it is nature that judges and will determine if the work of scientists is successful and true or has failed. In metaphor, the work of a scientist has been compared to the work of a tailor who measures, designs, and crafts the pieces of the garment he is making to fit the client perfectly, and when the garment seems to be finished, it is held up to the client to see if it fits.

In the metaphor, does the finished research project fit and explain the element of the natural, physical world that the scientist was investigating? After much testing in nature, if the results of the scientist's research explain and predict correctly the functions of his subject, his work is accepted and moves into the community of science.

Nobel laureate physicist Richard Feynman wrote an essay titled "The Value of Science," appearing in chapter 1 of *Frontiers in Science: A Survey*, Edward Hutchings Jr., editor (New York: Basic Books, 1958). My first book was published in 1981 by Princeton University Press. This essay was quite important to me. I read it many times, especially the paragraph below, where Feynman describes the feelings he experiences as he works on a research project and goes deeper and deeper into the study, finally finding an answer to his quest, only to discover that by his success he has uncovered an even deeper question. Remaining excited and elated, he calls this the "Grand Adventure."

It is true that few unscientific people have this particular type of religious experience. Our poets do not write about it; our artists do not try to portray this remarkable thing. I don't know why. Is nobody inspired by our present picture of the universe? The value of science remains unsung by singers, so you are reduced to hearing—not a song or a poem, but an evening lecture about it. This is not yet a scientific age.

Poets too are searching and exploring, asking questions, testing phrases, listening to the music of the language, studying the craft and the art of poetry.

They subject their work to testing, trusting the opinions of other poets who have acquired the skill to communicate and enlighten readers and listeners. Poets judge their own reactions to the words and the forms they have chosen. They reach out to informed critics and audiences, listen, and observe.

In his July 1991 *Scientific American* article, "Essay: The Poetry of Science," John Timpane writes:

> Early in [the 20th] century, an old and great Dilemma resurfaced—Poetry or Science? . . .
>
> In truth . . . 20th-century poets owed much to science. In giving poets more things to think about, more viewpoints to take, science enlarged the ambit of the imagination and bade the poet take over from there. . . .
>
> These two great ways of seeing lie on the same imaginative continuum. They do not compete; they connect. If science explicates the surprising, complex, undreamed of truth, poetry enacts the full impact of that truth on the human consciousness. A good poet can take an insight revealed by science and suggest the full range of its human importance.
>
> Poets writing at this very moment—some good ones are Gary Snyder, Albert Goldbarth, Elizabeth Socolow, Ed Dorn, A. R. Ammons and Pattiann Rogers—are doing just that.

In the arts in this year, 2022, many poets have made progress in portraying the recent discoveries about the universe and the earth, the births and the deaths, the beginnings and the endings in both realms, that scientists have given us. But expressions or questions of how deeply the human soul and heart are affected by this expanded vision of our world have not been revealed poetically in "the full range of its human importance."

In my work, I've endeavored to convey my fascination with the results of scientific research and what they continue to reveal to all of us, enlarging our vision, expanding our vocabulary, describing our physical universe—from the tiniest known elementary particle to the unending edge of the universe (or, at least, as far as we can calculate now), from the birth of light in our universe and the births of stars and galaxies to the birth of a butterfly. It is possible now to view the speed of the sperm, the penetration of the ovum, and the development of a human child in the womb. In what way do these enlarged visions and understandings affect the human heart, the spiritual soul? Reactions to discoveries that touch the heart and soul are largely the purview of artists who portray such reactions with their talents—not through a lecture, a dogma, a sermon, or a scree, but through a song, a symphony, a drama, a sculpture, a painting, or poems by poets engaging a bold imagination, employing all poetic crafts possible.

Finally, I believe the following words, from Stephen Jay Gould's 2002 book *The Structure of Evolutionary Theory*, perfectly present a combination of scientific and poetic skills enhancing and celebrating together an amazing perception:

> Something almost unspeakably holy—I don't know how else to say this—underlies our discovery and confirmation of the actual details that made our world and also, in realms of contingency, assured the minutiae of its construction in the manner we know, and not in any one of a trillion other ways, nearly all of which would not have included the evolution of a scribe to record the beauty, the cruelty, the fascination, and the mystery.

I don't call this last piece a poem, although the language is remarkably poetic and beautiful. I don't call it a prayer, as it does not bless nor implore. It is scientifically and emphatically stated and astonishingly true. The author has named it. I look out now from the earth at the sky and our world, and I agree.

# Essential Electrical Flickering and the Brain

## John A. Rogers

A healthy human brain operates through dynamic patterns of electrical impulses created and organized by neurons that exist in complex, three-dimensional networks. This electrical flickering sustains thoughts and memories, and it also controls a range of autonomous body functions, all the time, even during sleep.

Scientists can now precisely monitor and modulate these electrical patterns of activity to assess the health of the brain, to uncover fundamental aspects of brain function, and, in some cases, to repair damaged or injured brains.

The following three microscopic images illustrate modes for coupling man-made electronic devices with neural systems at three different length scales—from the entire human brain to small neural networks to individual neurons. Flickering in these devices couples with flickering of neural processes in elaborate ways that support applications ranging from diagnostic and therapeutic uses in clinical medicine to basic investigational purposes in neuroscience research.

These images make beautiful and unique patterns, unintentionally creating art through scientific exploration.

# I. The Human Brain

Flickering of neural activity across the surface of the prefrontal cortex induces flickering of electrical currents in metal mesh structures on the skin of the forehead.

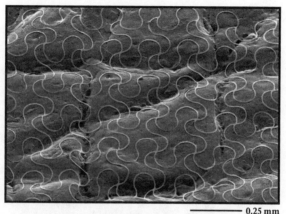

———— 0.25 mm

This image, captured with a scanning electron microscope, shows a filamentary serpentine mesh of metal traces resting on the textured surface of the skin of the forehead. Fluctuations in electrical potential associated with neural processes in the prefrontal cortex induce corresponding electrical currents that pass through the mesh. Sensing and recording the signals generated in this way represents a process known as electroencephalography. Applications range from brain-controlled interfaces for consumer electronic devices to diagnostic measurements for neurological disorders such as epilepsy.

> There is an untapped power of light
> lying dormant tonight in each crystal grasp
> in every flickering splinter of snow falling
> over the icy valleys of the Himalayas.

(FROM "LIGHTNING FROM LIGHTNING, I SAID," *WAYFARE*)

## II. Neural Networks

Flickering of neural activity across neural networks in an engineered "mini-brain" induce flickering electrical currents in metal electrodes distributed across ribbons that define a soft, basketlike supporting framework. Flickering voltages applied to these same electrodes stimulate corresponding network activity, in a programmable manner.

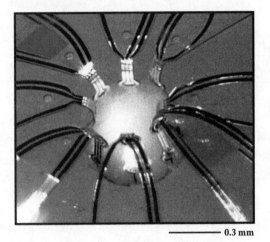

——————— 0.3 mm

This image, captured with an optical microscope, shows a three-dimensional framework of electrodes that envelops a millimeter-scale spherical tissue structure comprised of neurons grown from human stem cells, sometimes referred to as a mini-brain or cortical spheroid. Activity of neural networks in this spheroid generates electrical impulses that can be measured through the electrodes in a process analogous to electrocorticography. Electrical stimuli applied to the tissue through these same electrodes serve as the basis for controlling the behaviors of these networks. Applications range from fundamental studies of traumatic brain injuries to basic investigations of network formation associated with learning.

> Flickering: to make visible the art
> of light in motion on dew-covered
> vines of morning glories

(FROM "TO COME BACK," *HOLY HEATHEN RHAPSODY*)

# III. Neurons

Flickering of a cellular-scale light-emitting diode causes flickering activity of individual neurons that are genetically modified to respond to light.

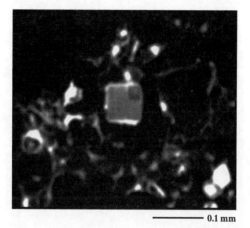

——————— 0.1 mm

This image, captured with an optical microscope, shows a cellular-scale light-emitting diode (LED) surrounded by a collection of individual neurons. Genetic modifications allow these cells to be activated or silenced by exposure to light, as the basis of a technique known as optogenetics. Applications of this method in neuroscience research reveal underlying mechanisms associated with neural activity and, by extension, the foundational principles that define brain function.

> The silent, solemn moon, bound
> in its flight alone far above the peaks,
> far above the earth, is surrounded there
> forever by bevies of giddy stars,
> all asparkling, all aflickering, all aglow.

(FROM "THE ESTATE OF SOLEMNITY," *QUICKENING FIELDS*)

# Notes and Poems

All the poems appearing in this book were written by Pattiann Rogers. A few poems, slightly modified, are composed of lines taken from poems written by Pattiann Rogers and published in her books by Penguin Books between the years of 2010 and 2022.

The black-winged beetles of the order Coleoptera,
those fireflies gliding, almost floating, through
every space in the forest, above the dank debris
and murk of the earth, into the upper canopies
igniting the wild bioluminescence, each one
flickering with passion, drawing us like spirits
into the insect art of their being.

(FROM "THE STORY HUNT: MISSOURI COUNTRYSIDE, JUNE 2010,"
*HOLY HEATHEN RHAPSODY*)

When the lantern begins to flicker and dim
deep in the cave, fades, fails, and we are crawling now,
hands and knees on damp rock. All the cells
of our bodies—gut, brain, fingertips, hair on end—-
are straining to see. The nose sniffs for light.

(FROM "VULNERABLE AND SUSCEPTIBLE,"
*HOLY HEATHEN RHAPSODY*)

Down the switch backs,
toward the flapping sea flickering and singing
like flocks of meadow birds at dawn.

(FROM "BY AND BY, BY AND BY," *WAYFARE*)


They float and sweep. They flicker
and unfold having neither electrons
nor atoms, neither grasp nor escape.
Like skeletons they could be scaffolds.
They are visible echoes.

(FROM "THE DOXOLOGY OF SHADOWS,"
*HOLY HEATHEN RHAPSODY*)

# Acknowledgments

My gratitude and thanks to the editors, staff, and students for their dedication to the journals below and their continuing publication of new literature, prose, and poetry:

*AGNI*: "Keeping Beauty under Control"

*American Literary Review*: "The Perfect Lover"

*Clockwatch Review*: "Making Love with the Gods"

*Copper Nickel*: "Archetype II," "The Artist"

*Iron Horse Literary Review*: "The Knocking"

*The Manhattan Review*: "Assessing the Situation: Breath, Spirit, and Chickadees," "In Place, in Time," "Never Alone," "The Skedaddlers, an Overview"

*Tampa Review*: "Stranger and Stranger"

*Terrain.org*: "Of Rivers or Trees?"

My thanks to the editors of the following chapbooks in which certain poems in this book appeared: *The Only Holy Window* (Trilobite Press, 1984) and *Summer's Company* (Brooding Heron Press, 2009).

I want to thank the sponsoring organizations and all those who worked to keep poetry alive and public during the COVID-19 pandemic. Thank you for bringing people together remotely for live readings of poems and discussions with the poets.

A special thanks to those who invited me to participate in the following remote poetry reading events:

Nathan P. Carson, director, FPU Wilderness Programs, a Zoom event for the forthcoming anthology *Virtue, Vice & Eco Flourishing.*

The Hudson Valley Writers Center, Jennifer Franklin, Manager, and Tina Kelley.

*Alaska Quarterly Review*, a reading for the second annual *Pièces de Résistance*, a virtual reading series hosted by the Anchorage Museum, Ronald Spatz, editor, *Alaska Quarterly Review*.

The Sowell Virtual Reading Series, Diane Warner, librarian for the James Sowell Family Collection in Literature, Community, and the Natural World, Texas Tech University.

Although I was unable to attend in person the Poets for Science exhibit at the Pratt Museum in Homer, Alaska, I appreciated the invitation to have my poem exhibited along with the other poems hung on the Listening Wall in the museum. I thank Jane Hirshfield for the invitation, her work in organizing this event, and her assistance in having my poem read aloud by a member of the Wick Poetry Center.

Professor John A. Rogers, my son, is the author of "Essential Electrical Flickering and the Brain." He contributed the three images displayed, described, and explained in his text. It was a pleasure to work together with him. Thank you, John, for the time and knowledge you gave to this project. I couldn't have ventured into it or completed it without you.

My husband, John R. Rogers, was a welcome assistant in editing the manuscript. He was especially helpful to me as a proofreader and a part-time typist and was always nearby with solutions when computer problems arose. Thank you, John, for your skills, patience, and constant support.

Paul Slovak, my editor and friend, has been present and engaged from the beginning of *Flickering*. He added suggestions in the organizations of the poems in the manuscript and gave advice about the final section and was also tolerant and generous with the requests and suggestions that my son and I offered. We all listened and worked together as a team, depending on Paul's experience and knowledge of what was possible and what was required in the process of putting the manuscript together and shaping the way it evolved into the unique book that it is. Thank you, Paul. Your presence was vital in our endeavors and will always be greatly appreciated.

**Pattiann Rogers** has published fifteen books of poetry and two collections of essays. Her most recent books are the poetry collections *Quickening Fields* (Penguin, 2017) and *Holy Heathen Rhapsody* (Penguin, 2013). *Song of the World Becoming: New and Collected Poems, 1981–2001* (Milkweed Editions) was a finalist for the Los Angeles Times Book Prize. *Firekeeper: New and Selected Poems* was a finalist for the Lenore Marshall Poetry Prize. Rogers is the recipient of the John Burroughs Medal for Lifetime Achievement in Nature Poetry (2018), the College of Arts and Science Distinguished Alumni Award from the University of Missouri (2022), two NEA Grants, a Guggenheim Fellowship, a 2005 Literary Award in Poetry from the Lannan Foundation, and five Pushcart Prizes. Her work has appeared in *The Best American Poetry* twice, and in *The Best Spiritual Writing* five times. In May 2000, Rogers was in residence at the Rockefeller Foundation's Bellagio Center in Bellagio, Italy. She was associate professor at the University of Arkansas from 1993 to 1997. Rogers's papers are archived in the Sowell Family Collection of Literature, Community, and the Natural World at Texas Tech University. She is the mother of two sons and has three grandsons. She lives with her husband, a retired geophysicist, in Colorado.

✳

**John A. Rogers** is the Louis Simpson and Kimberly Querrey Professor of Materials Science and Engineering, Biomedical Engineering, and Medicine at Northwestern University. He earned his PhD in physical chemistry at Massachusetts Institute of Technology in 1995. He spent the early part of his career at Bell Laboratories and then at the University of Illinois at Urbana-Champaign. Among other significant recognitions, he is a MacArthur Fellow and has been given the Smithsonian American Ingenuity Award in the Physical Sciences, the Benjamin Franklin Medal from the Franklin Institute, and a Guggenheim Fellowship. He is one of roughly two dozen people in history to have been elected to all three U.S. national academies: the National Academy of Engineering, the National Academy of Sciences, and the National Academy of Medicine. He has created more than one hundred patented inventions, including a very small wireless device designed to monitor the health of premature babies without interfering wires and adhesives that can damage their fragile skin and complicate even basic aspects of clinical care. This device also allows parents to freely cuddle their child, the warmth and touch of a human body being very important in the healthy development of an infant during these early days of life.

# PENGUIN POETS

# PENGUIN POETS

PHILLIS LEVIN
*May Day*
*Mercury*
*Mr. Memory & Other Poems*

PATRICIA LOCKWOOD
*Motherland Fatherland*
  *Homelandsexuals*

WILLIAM LOGAN
*Rift of Light*

J. MICHAEL MARTINEZ
*Museum of the Americas*

ADRIAN MATEJKA
*The Big Smoke*
*Map to the Stars*
*Mixology*
*Somebody Else Sold the World*

MICHAEL MCCLURE
*Huge Dreams: San Francisco*
  *and Beat Poems*

ROSE MCLARNEY
*Forage*
*Its Day Being Gone*

DAVID MELTZER
*David's Copy: The Selected*
  *Poems of David Meltzer*

TERESA K. MILLER
*Borderline Fortune*

ROBERT MORGAN
*Dark Energy*
*Terroir*

CAROL MUSKE-DUKES
*Blue Rose*
*An Octave Above Thunder:*
  *New and Selected Poems*
*Red Trousseau*
*Twin Cities*

ALICE NOTLEY
*Certain Magical Acts*
*Culture of One*
*The Descent of Alette*
*Disobedience*
*For the Ride*
*In the Pines*
*Mysteries of Small Houses*

WILLIE PERDOMO
*The Crazy Bunch*
*The Essential Hits of Shorty*
  *Bon Bon*

DANIEL POPPICK
*Fear of Description*

LIA PURPURA
*It Shouldn't Have Been*
  *Beautiful*

LAWRENCE RAAB
*The History of Forgetting*

BARBARA RAS
*The Last Skin*
*One Hidden Stuff*

MICHAEL ROBBINS
*Alien vs. Predator*
*The Second Sex*
*Walkman*

PATTIANN ROGERS
*Flickering*
*Generations*
*Holy Heathen Rhapsody*
*Quickening Fields*
*Wayfare*

SAM SAX
*Madness*

ROBYN SCHIFF
*A Woman of Property*

WILLIAM STOBB
*Absentia*
*Nervous Systems*

TRYFON TOLIDES
*An Almost Pure Empty*
  *Walking*

VINCENT TORO
*Tertulia*

PAUL TRAN
*All the Flowers Kneeling*

SARAH VAP
*Viability*

ANNE WALDMAN
*Gossamurmur*
*Kill or Cure*
*Manatee/Humanity*
*Trickster Feminism*

JAMES WELCH
*Riding the Earthboy 40*

PHILIP WHALEN
*Overtime: Selected Poems*

PHILLIP B. WILLIAMS
*Mutiny*

ROBERT WRIGLEY
*Anatomy of Melancholy and*
  *Other Poems*
*Beautiful Country*
*Box*
*Earthly Meditations:*
  *New and Selected Poems*
*Lives of the Animals*
*Reign of Snakes*
*The True Account of Myself as*
  *a Bird*

MARK YAKICH
*The Importance of Peeling*
  *Potatoes in Ukraine*
*Spiritual Exercises*
*Unrelated Individuals Forming*
  *a Group Waiting to Cross*